Journey of the Medicine Man

This is such a strong book, written in a strong plain style. Red Hawk is like Whitman because he can contain multitudes and yet he is always so authentically himself. Behind all these [poems] there is always one single simple thing, which is Red Hawk's own voice. Haunting and stark, ironic and spare.

These poems are desperately important to us all today because Red Hawk has that rarest of all virtues (Virgil had it, Dante had it, Shakespeare had it) — a sense of civilization, something most of us have forgotten all about. Behind each of these miraculously crafted poems, Red Hawk speaks of the wise silence and the raw courage and the animal honesty and the elemental pride we will all be needing if we are to survive on this godforsaken planet as free men and women.

William Packard, editor emeritus
New York Quarterly

Journey of the Medicine Man
Red Hawk

August House/Little Rock

A NONPROFIT ORGANIZATION FOR THE WRITTEN ARTS

ISBN 0-935304-62-2 Hardback
ISBN 0-935304-63-0 Quality Paperback

Library of Congress Catalog Card No. 83-70537

First Edition, November, 1983.

This book was published by August House, Inc., a
nonprofit organization for the written arts in
Arkansas. No government funds have been used in
this publication. By your purchase of August House
books and memberships, you make possible the
publication of new Arkansas books and the
preservation of Arkansas's literary heritage.

The hardback edition of this August House book is
printed on acid-free paper, the expected shelf life of
which is four hundred years, depending upon the
environment in which it is shelved.

For Little Wind
and Rain Drop, Dust-in-the-Wind
For Bhagwan
With awe and devotion

Acknowledgements

Poetry: "How I Love You," "Master, Master, Lord of the Dance"

The New York Quarterly: "Brujo," "Learning the Language of Stones"

The Kansas Quarterly

The Hiram Poetry Review

Practicing Midwife: "Young Midwife's First Stillbirth," "Old Midwife Delivering"

The Southern Poetry Review

The Rocky Mountain Review

The Wisconsin Review

The Western Humanities Review

Thicket

Pudding

Pteranadon

The Arkansas Democrat

The Arkansas Times

Equinox

"The Gunfighter" won Grand Prize, Natl. Fed. State Poetry Societies

The publisher and author would like to express their gratitude for the contributions of these artists: David R. Greene, for his illustrations on the cover and on pages 58 and 77; Pearl-Breathes-The-World, for her illustration on page 2; David Jacobs, for the photography in the book; and Ira Hocut, for the production artwork.

Table of Contents

Prologue

Journey of the Medicine Man

i. Down from the mountain
    the red hawk glides,
    into the land of the Dreamer
    who puts all men to sleep with words
    and breaks their hearts with dreaming.

    Among ten thousand sleeping men
    one hawk waking;
    among ten thousand dreaming faces
    two hawk eyes gazing;
    among ten thousand broken hearts
    one hawk heart healing.

ii. Straight for the Dreamer
    the red hawk sails.
    With silence
    he strikes the Dreamer down,
    scattering words like pieces of fire.

Among ten thousand words
one silence;
among ten thousand raging torrents
one still pool;
among ten thousand broken hearts
one heart rejoicing.

iii. Now there is a stillness in leaf and bone
and the red hawk soars from the dream of death.
The moment the mountain touches him
he is a man again
and offers prayers of feather, pipe and stone.

On a single patient mountain
one man going slow;
on a single watchful boulder
one man paying attention;
in the single grateful heart
one man kneeling, giving thanks.

i: Fear

Variations on the Theme of Darkness

i.   High in the mountains
     snow has fallen deep
     as an old man's eyes going out;
     the black hollow of his mouth
     swallows the sun.
     The mountain wears deep snow
     uneasily.

ii. If the shadow of a crow
     crosses the belly of a pregnant woman
     her child's face will be stained
     by dark water rising in moonlight.

iii. The crow's shadow is torn from him
     as he crosses high mountain snow.
     He circles helplessly against the white,
     blindly seeking his mark.
     An old man swallows him.

iv. The fetus strains against membrane
as the water rises
staining its face.

v. When night stretches over cold water
like the shadow of a lost crow,
a single cry can roll for miles
across the snow
and swallow an old man.

Picture of Grandmother
Found in my Father's Old Wallet

Oh my god,
her eyes stop blood.
They demand payment from everyone.
My father is the small boy
who stands beside her in shorts.
He is terrified.
He is holding her small black hat,
fingering the long hatpin with a pearl on the end.
If they had not snapped the picture
I believe he would have killed her then.
Between myself and my grandmother
there is little physical resemblance,
but many have said I sometimes look like my father.
I believe it is when I am
terribly afraid;
it is just before I do my mother in.

In the Alcoholic Ward

Piss smell in the floorboards.
No whiskey here.
Father has made sure;
he went on hands and knees into every room,
praying some weak-willed drunk had broken the rules.
No one had
so he drank lighter fluid and turpentine
he found in the janitor's closet.
They first let us see him a month later
after he started shock treatments.
When the head nurse wheeled him in
his eyes were as still as murder.
Even now they tell about the last night:
how he somehow got to the lighter fluid again
and made his way to the staff barracks;
how he beat the head nurse with her own cat
and, flushed with success,
went out by standing in her toilet,
unscrewing the overhead bulb,
and sticking his finger in the socket.

Somehow, the cat survived.

For Susan, Who Could Not Play Brahms

To truly give love you must accept death
but it is hard when you know
the way Susan went.
Her husband sold insurance
and went with other women,
so Susan started hanging out along the tracks
drinking wine with the Indians.

They still tell how
one night when she was no drunker than usual
Susan stood quietly watching the spotlight
of a fast freight;
and how she stepped calmly onto the track,
one arm raised in a casual goodbye,
and walked right into the engine.
When we went to tell her husband
he would not come to the door
lest we interrupt the Brahms he was playing.

To truly give love you must keep things in perspective
but it is hard when you know
how full the world is of insurance men
who can play Brahms,
and how few women there are
who would walk into a fast freight
for the man they love.

Most People Will Blindly Follow Any Asshole

For years now
I've been doing a little work on myself,
nothing much
just watching my thoughts
listening to the craziness closely
keeping my body still,
just some small things.

What it has shown me mainly
is that every kind of asshole
you could possibly think of
I am
and I am them over and over
in my thoughts.

This knowledge has produced
some noticeable changes
in my behavior

such that many people,
who are desperate and afraid,
want to make much more of me than
I am
and confuse me with my Betters.

Take tonight for example:
Pearl, who mistakes me for my Betters,
came up to my screened porch;
     Does the master want any company
she said
when all there was was this asshole
sitting there on the porch
writing this poem.

The Old Ones Who Remember Me are Gone

Everyone who knew me here is dead.
Now that I can do anything
and not ruin the name nobody knows
I'm too old to do it.
I have no reputation;
it lies with the old ones
in Willow Creek Cemetery
and they don't even mow the grass there anymore.

Fame is a bawd,
reputation a fraud.

The stones at Willow Creek tumble,
disappear in tall grass,
decay.
So do I.

The Married Woman's Dream

There is a harmony of blackbirds at dawn,
their golden eyes uncertain as a shaking pond.
She rises naked and singing,
wraps herself in unbraided hair,
and descends in her morning flesh to the lawn.
Her nipples are stiff and stinging
with cold.
Her lover rises from the flock,
wrapping her body in wings
so fine they would tear
like an old
woman's skin
if she were not so soft
and shaking with love.
If she were a bird
I would have her fly away with him,
but she does not believe her possibilities.
In the half-light she stumbles
and goes to her knees,
her hair floating around her like feathers.
She wants to scream at the dark line of birds
as they circle and climb the red sky.
In a moment she will awaken in her bed,
wet and exhausted,
her nipples raw.

You see?
She cannot explain the black feather
clutched in her fist.

Sakura, Sakura: Cherry Blossoms
(for Kimio Eto)

In the still pool
moonlight carves itself like a ribbon
of bright blood
feeding a dark stream.
Cherry blossoms float like a dream,
their fleshy petals riding the flood;
the soft wind stays hidden
in the leaf. The air is cool
and the maiden weeping alongside
the pool is chilled and very
still. Today she was a child bride.
The air is heavy with cherry.

Learning the Language of Stones

They speak through their humps mainly,
splitting them open
to reveal feathers
and thick blood.

They have not forgotten
the human in them;
though they rarely speak of it,
sometimes one will groan

as he breaks loose from the rest
and goes thundering down the slope,
crushing trees,
and hurls himself into the river.

After that,
the silence.

ii: Clarity_____

Living Alone

I think of women often
and like waking up next to one.
Yet when they are gone
there is the single brown reed
still shaking above the frozen lake,
bending in the wind.
If the water doesn't get much colder
I think I can make it
until the first thaw.

Sunday Evening

Sunday is the day of the dead
for divorced men;
it is the day I take my children home.
I hold them dearly to me
with a kiss that longs for eternity,
and walk away.
Sunday is the Sabbath
and I keep it wholly
apart from living things:
it is the day of goodbyes;
the day of the dark solitude descending;
the day of the futility of kisses;
the day I stop and wave from the corner
and as the cold wind shifts south,
turn for my apartment
like a man alone in a snowy forest
turns to face oncoming wolves.

Ghazal for my Students

I have planted turnips by moonlight and heard them call out.
Now I work in a dark, stranger soil and the calls do not stop.

Here, mules must still be driven to learn
and are often found dead in their traces.

Better to fling seed on stone and pray for a miracle
than to follow a plowed furrow a single lifetime.

The planet is the sacred classroom;
all who come there are honored.

The sin of the drifter is having a direction.
The sin of the teacher is having an answer.

Do not come to me expecting truths;
I too am darkness seeking a star.

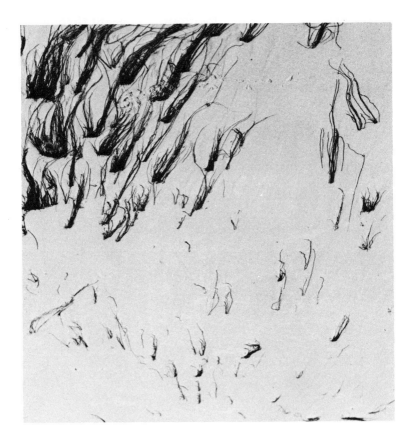

Ghazal for Fathers

A man produces more than 200 million sperm in a day,
one of which alters the path of his star forever.

In the night, my daughter's cry awakens me;
I prepare to give my life.

Rain Drop, my youngest, asks me to sing her lullabies;
I enchant the darkness, desperately keeping it from her.

Little Wind, my oldest, loves and worships me
as if it were I who made her.

Even now, two people are raising the husband of my daughter.
Dear God, let them be gentle and full of love.

I dreamt I saw my daughters drift away;
when I awoke I stabbed my eyes.

At the Supposed Site of Troy

There is no evidence of a body
having been dragged in circles over stones,
nor of spearheads, a remnant of gold armor,
or near the water, some piece of burned wood.

Where scholars are digging, flashes of light
jump from the blades of shovels, and men
knee-deep in the barren earth go wild
when they find a chamber pot. Achilles

would have let Patroclus lie with his face
frozen in this wretched soil forever
if he had known that withered men in shorts
would go to their knees in knobby wonder

at some fat damsel's toilet. Helen's face
was wasted in the desolation of this place.
She must have had a goat-herd's taste
to leave the golden throne of Menelaus

and like a gorgeous worm, be carried off
by a rotten apple. If their hot bodies grappled
under the rainy trees on this stone-swept spit,
they had neither fun, nor the hope of it.

The gods must have looked endlessly to find
a singer of the deeds that happened here;
one who could sing a pure song of pride and fear,
and still, perchance, just happened to be blind.

The Professors Gather After the Poetry Reading

They can't keep their mouths shut
they are so desperate,
so fearful of silence.
They want to make a show for their women,
they want to dream they are real.
They are like the great apes
making a display
to ward off a foe.

Soon I excuse myself,
go out on the balcony alone.
One of the women follows,
stands silently next to me.
She takes my hand and kisses it,
places it wordlessly on her breast,
looks at me without fear.

She is much stronger than the men,
has the courage of her action,
the wisdom of her silence.
I lift her skirt to feel her buttocks,
the muscles of her thigh.

There is no urgency between us,
no move to go further.
She had something to say to me
and I replied,
nothing more.

Back inside the professors wave their drinks,
talk louder.
What they cannot understand is
that there is one among them
who is wise,
a woman of courage,
something real,
something speechless and eloquent
standing there by the punchbowl.

The Stages of Man

The seed-bearer,
He forever seeks fertile ground;
He does not see
He is the fertile ground.

The wanderer,
He casts the seed in barren wastes;
He labors in vain
and does not work the soil.

The disciple,
He husbands the seed
and the fallow soil rests;
doing Nothing, He labors well.

The Master works the fertile soil,
sharecropping for the landlord:
He plows and then He sows,
He nurtures and He reaps.

Our Young Poets Had Better Be Strong

The trees grow tired
of churning out little magazines
full of young poets
desperate to be reborn in print;
the trees are weary
like the poems of the old poets
who refuse to see that a word
will not heal the sickness in their hearts
nor end the sorrow of the days
which comes each morning
the moment they awaken.

Very soon the trees will give out
and our young poets had better be strong then
because they will be the first to go.
Only the oldest and weariest ones
will be in print then;
they will lack the nobility of spirit
to be still
as the last trees groan
and smash their faces against the Earth.
Only the old and weary poets will refuse to see
that the last poem on the printed page

will not shade them from the heat
nor stand tall enough to catch the wind.
Then the young ones will have to relearn
singing their songs to soothe a handful
huddled together for warmth and courage;
they will have to be satisfied
that once in a great while
there will be a song so fine
it will be repeated for a thousand years
before it fades away;
our young poets had better be strong then.

Towards the Glorious Sun of Infinity
(for Robbie Basho)

The mind of the warrior
is afloat in its silence
like the red sun setting in the furthest trees;
his left hand blooms in the dying light

and he does not hope to see the dawn.
The forest sings itself to darkness
and the stone holds a light
he can feel in his palm;

it is the same light animals leave
on the stones along the river
where they have passed the night.
He thinks the wind

and it is in his hair;
he thinks the moon afloat
in its silence;
and he does not hope to see the dawn.

iii: Power_____

Brujo

i. If they have ever seen me
   it is because I once opened my shirt quickly before them
   and let them glimpse the hawk's feathers beneath,
   but that was long ago when I was young
   and still believed I was no fool
   and could prove it with a show of colors.

ii. Real magic is easy:
    to fly, for example,
    all I need do is imagine the trees
    from a different perspective;
    to disappear, I simply fly
    until I am not here.

iii. I once walked 50 miles in the dark
     until my blisters bled
     to kill a man.
     When I reached him he was sleeping
     and I turned away.
     Between any 2 humans, a gesture is important.

iv. In this life I have loved 4 women well
     and yet in the house of a stranger
     I went with the spirit of his wife
     to the basement where she had shot herself
     and then I knew that one day
     I would be this old and alone.

 v. If they have ever seen me
     it is because I once flew in through the window
     and stood there as if they could see,
     but I was an old man then and knew
     that at any moment a fool will risk everything
     because he has nothing to gain.

An Inquiry Into Art
(for Robert Pirsig)

The idea
is to catch the moment
and dance;
to look at the world
from both sides
like the farmer in Iowa
who glances up from his plow,
startled,
believing he has just caught a scent
of the ocean;
looking up he sees instead
rain clouds
and shakes his head,
smiling;
at his first nod
a gull bends brightly out
on a band of wind,
dancing in a haze of rain.

He looks to heaven
and his face fills with rain,
his hair floats on air,
his shirt billows and gasps.
He rises
and flies west.

All Things Must Pass
(for George Harrison)

The angel coming through the palace window
has knocked the water vase on the sill;
it trembles,
the water shaking like timid love.

The pale, raven-haired woman sitting by the still pool
changes instantly to a Calcutta whore,
her stall infested with vermin.
She tires of knocking them from her naked sweating body.
Her bright red lips are badly bruised.

In seven years she buys her way out
and works as a porter on the road to Bombay,
forever saving her money;
her skin is lined like a parchment map.
She longs for the children in her palace.

One day she sits exhausted on a windowsill
and is instantly pale and raven-haired,
idling in her silk gown by the still pool;
she lunges to grab the vase before it topples.

The Gunfighter

A gunfighter is barely hidden in my artful shadow.
As I bend owlishly over a new poem, he hunches
     crosslegged
over the heavy smell of brass casings and mounds of
     powder.
His fingers as supple as a new wound, he carefully mixes

various colored powders into the cupping brass like a poet
loving his words into weapons. As he softly fits the tight
     lead head,
he lines bullets row upon row in front of his anxious gun
and stares at the poem on my page, his knuckles popping
     like shots

in the sullen room. As I revise a new poem he fingers his
     gun
gently under a bright light and begins to break it down,
brushing each piece with a fine horsehair brush and
     spreading
a thin film of oil over the tender metal until it gives
     whispers

of light into his still eyes. When the gun is put together
he weighs it solidly in his careful hand, closing his eyes
as he sights with his fingertips along the cylinder, his breath
shining as it smokes the polished metal. Before I go to a
     reading

he will stand for hours, first at the window, his fists
     clenching
and unclenching as he draws deep, steady breaths. Then
he will slip on tight leather gloves, tie down his holster,
and stand easily before the mirror. He will clench his fist

at his chest, drop it slowly until it is just above his gun,
and then unclench it as fast as a snake's head striking.
He never touches the gun, only nods to himself, rolls a
    cigarette,
and walks out into the sunlight without a word.

As I read, he has the drop on everyone. He seldom shoots;
only rarely, a line will set him off, he will move like a wolf
to people's sides, his hand will draw within a whisper of
    shaking,
and as I read, he will calmly blow them out of their chairs.

Time is an Eternity of Small Heroes

All his life, Grandfather worked the tops
of the giant sledge ovens without a mask,
breathing sulphur.
Because he was strong and honest,
years ago the mill men elected him
to work the steam whistle
that thundered at the drop of noon.
Since an oven jockey with sulphur lungs
has no concept of power,
each day just before noon
he would call the city hall operator
to get the official time.
What he could not know
crawling from the suffocating sky
to make his way to the phone,
was that every day as his whistle
shattered the smoky stillness of noon,
everyone in town, including
the city hall operator,
set his clock.

Mizu No Hentai: Water Transformations

i. As the white bird brushes the wet leaf,
    the moon opens like a bright petal,
    waiting for the feather to shine.

    Rain hides its face;
    as it comes across the mountain
    dark nostrils breathe the moon.

    The sky during rain
    is like the dark drop of blood
    on your lip during love.

ii. High in the mountains,
    the brown reed pins deep snow against the sky,
    holding back the flood.

    Snow longs for the coming of spring;
    it covers the feathers of the white bird
    torn by the silver fox.

    The sky during snow
    is like your face wrapped in damp hair
    as you roll your head on my pillow.

iii. Beneath the ice
     the black water trembles,
     longing to touch the snow.

     Ice is the patient one;
     after ten thousand centuries
     it inches mutely toward the city.

     The sky mirrored in ice
     is like your body floating in my eyes,
     one slow leg lazily rolling.

The Old Blind Elephant

Once in a while
among the young bulls,
one feels
that old Dark Eyes
can be taken.

Just one,
once in a while,
is enough
to teach them.

The Way of Power

I will tell you how it is with Power.
The Way is hard
and easily lost.

Take me for example.
Once I had a tiny power
no greater than the breath of a bird,
the power to make words.
But it was more than I could handle.

I was sloppy with it:
spoke too much
and at the wrong times;
used the poems badly
for my own glory.

So the Power was taken away.
Even the breath of a bird
made me vain and arrogant
and I used it to make myself little.

Now I sit still on my porch
and I see how
I am a stupid man
who was made sick
by the bird's breath.

I am dying of it
because the breath got inside me
before I made myself strong
and now it is blowing me away
like a small bird without strength
caught in a high wind.

What is left for me
is to die quietly
because my stupidity made a big noise.
This is what I know
about Power.

iv: Death _____

The Young Midwife's First Stillbirth
(for Dusty)

"Be still and know..." Jesus

Sooner or later it happens,
the midwives are seasoned by death.
It breaks them all
but the strong ones heal,
grow wise and solid like great stones
rooted in a forest floor.

So it was nothing new, except to her.
The still child stopped her
and she held it in her hands.
The wide stare
snared her;
she fell for the quiet face.
Then death had her.
It shook her hard
from tooth to bone
and she held it in her hands.
It broke her,
then it put her back together
and she held it in her hands.

When death finished with her
she was changed:
now she startles people with her fierce dark beauty,
her rude and muscular animal grace
like a lone female wolf
who has survived a hard winter;
now she is so still it scares the talkers
because she does not fall for words.
Now she is like the forest at sunrise:
a stillness giving birth,
being born.

Old Man Carving Stone

He serves the stone
and the stone shapes him:
it has taught him to go slow,
to pay attention;
he has learned to be amazed.
He will hold a proper stone for days,
sitting patiently and smoking his pipe,
waiting for the stone
to reveal its form;
his hands do the rest.
He is no longer fooled
that he is the maker;
he allows the stone to use him.
In return
it shows him how to die:
patiently,
face full of sunlight,
bathed in rain, dried in wind,
slowly, slowly
wearing away.

Is This the Best You Have to Show Me, Mister Death?

Just before my mother died, Death first strolled out
from behind me and showed his face,
his yellow eyes blank as sandstones
as he danced and strutted on her ragged breath.

Is this the best you have to show me, Mister Death,
making an old, beaten woman's breath rattle
while her eyes go out?
Save your best for me, Yellow Eyes,

for I wear my dying like a coat of sunlight,
and will dance when I am covered up with night;
you will find me wandering in the woods,
singing myself to death.

The Walrus-Poet
(for Bill Wantling)

If you stand huddled in the rocks,
protected from the wind and spray
along the coast of Greenland,
you will see day after day
great fat walruses washed onto the rocks.
They lie glistening obesely in the sun
snorting.
Sometimes the heat and comfort
arouse them sexually;
they have their way with young female sea-pups
and blubber saintly about in their fat kingdoms.
One somehow was washed ashore in the Midwest
disguised as a fat poet
and the shock of such a sight in Illinois
led the natives to worship him for awhile.
It was an affair doomed to brevity;
the need for walrus blubber
to light the lamps of ruined Illinois towns
soon overcame their need for song.
Friends managed to save
only the ponderous ivory tusks
but on certain days when the light hits them
through the cornfields
they gleam and dance like white birds in flight
or like thin curved tuna breaking surface
on an arc of spray.
It is all we have;
some say the beast was never among us.

When I Am Dead

When I am dead
my daughters will glimpse me crossing their faces
as they stare in the mirror.
They will discover me with a start of joy
in the eyes of their newborn.
Generations of lovers
will roll their heads softly off the pillow,
loving my face
without ever knowing my name.
And when their children stand alone
in the still and fearful cold
they will not know I loved their mother's mother
or that it is my voice keening on the wind,
yet they will be full of me;
they will not know that I was a man,
yet I am preparing them to be alone
and I will never leave them.

Young Woman on Her Wedding Night

Her eyes are wild
like oat seeds in a high wind
and the soft slip
she lifts over her head
consumes her.

Her body is nipple pink
and tender
as she looks away,
one hand covering her down,
the other lifting her breast to him.

The moon drifts at the open window
like a petal on a still pond
and catches in the slender tree.
When she is old and alone,

dying in her room,
she will bathe again in that moonlight
and open to the one
that comes to take her.

The Note Granddad Left When He Disappeared

If you have to come after me
bury me there
just the way you find me,
wrapped in the horse blanket Dusty wove,
holding my red stone pipe.
If a stranger finds the body,
don't claim it;
it is no longer mine
and I am walking away from it
right now.

The White Man

Let him see who really owns the land
when he slips on the rocks
and his death slaps him sideways
so his tongue lies broken
between his teeth;
let him see when he cannot rise
from the ground he owns
and the wolves tear him;
let him see when they turn
from what remains of his body,
their tongues dripping from their mouths
like cheap ribbon,
and the first summer the bones bleach;
the second they are chalk;
the third, wild grasses brush in the wind.

Let him see then.

Old Midwife, Delivering
(for Dusty)

Her loving hands are with child;
at the end of the solitary journey
the head blooms in her gentle fingers
like a fragile seed flowering.
With silence
she delivers the race.
Her hands are the first teaching.

Then she rises.
From a small bag
she takes a stone pipe, cradles,
fills it tenderly.
She has seen many children come,
pass through her fingers like smoke,
burn brightly and die out.

She sits quietly
and smokes.

Wind Over the Earth

Like the Earth,
the wise man speaks no word
when his heart is full.

If his mind is a hollow reed
then the skin of his lover sings
beneath her silk robe
as she enters his room;

breath dances between them
like wind over the Earth,
a harmony of silences.

When the heart of the wise man is full
silence is his adoration,
like the hollow reed
bowing in the wind.

Bridge of Sighs

When the river is between us
and the days drift away
like geese flying west,
I do not long for you:
I have seen how love dies
from desire,
wasting the moment
as if it were a lasting blaze
instead of a candle going out.
So I sit by the river
until the wind sighs
through the distant trees,
and then I speak your name.
If you sit by the river
you can hear me calling;
send your answer on a stone
tumbling through the clear, cold water
and I will find it early in the morning
as I go down to bathe.

When the river is between us,
I do not long for you.

How I Love You

It has just rained.
Humps gleam in the sun.
Dung steams.
The prairie is all buffalo for miles
and the great herd is uneasy.
Their pawing causes the ground to tremble
20 miles to the east in Topeka.

His huge head sharply up,
a great bull stands over his calving mate
at a distance from the rest of the herd.
As wind whispers in the prairie grass
he nuzzles his mate's belly softly,
his wet nostrils flaring.
The wind carries wolf.

Raising his head
he makes the slightest shift
surely and without hesitation;
a decision to sacrifice.
Flank shivers spread for miles like waves
across an ocean of wet fur.
The bulls move to the edge of a forming circle.
Suddenly
there are the wolves,
dozens of them,
clearing the first slight rise,
their bared teeth sprouting in the sun like ivory knives.
At that instant they see the great lone bull
moving in front of his mate
and they know what they are in for.
They almost stop.

Master, Master, Lord of the Dance
(for Dusty)

I follow the fox's trail
of drifting chicken feathers
into deep snow,
across the stock pond with the early sun
frozen in its eye.

Where the forest turns up the mountain
I hesitate:
as I left the house,
your kiss was full of tongue
and you held 4 cold, brown-speckled eggs
to my cheek;

on the other hand
the fox now has 2 of our 6 laying hens
and his courage is like a dark-eyed woman
coming in broad daylight
to steal the heart of a man.

As I turn back over the frozen pond
you top the low hill from the house,
running the snowy field to meet me;
your breath streams in your dark hair.
Two feathers blow across the ice
dancing in their early morning ecstasy.

Old Indian Woman's Lament for her Son

You have come a long way Black Crow
and I did not see you right away,
until you filled your dark wings with sunlight
and the day fell under your feathers;
I have come a long way too Black Crow,
and it has been dangerous for me
crossing the river of dreams
armed only with old age
and an old woman's dream:
to hold the body of my son once more
and hide the rag of my face in his hair.
Let the young woman use her beauty for comfort,
yet it is a brief shadow
and will not carry her very far toward death;
I grow old and would hold your head
until I have no breath
and ask nothing in return.
Instead I will walk 20 miles toward morning
to glimpse you skimming the lake,
two wings rising and two falling away
as they drip light from the first low trees.
That will be enough.

Ah, Black Crow   Black Crow

The Wheat Farmer Says Goodbye to His Only Daughter

His heart cracks like parched Earth
to see her go,
but he is not free enough to weep,
so he walks with her this evening
out in the summer wheat
where the stalks beat softly.

Suddenly, in his fertile anguish,
his heart blooms
and like the last mad king of wild wheat
he grabs his child and twirls her,
through the sea of grain he whirls her,
she holding tight, he boldly dancing
in the moonlight.
When at last they fall
he is winded and amazed,
on his knees embraces her.

And then she takes her leaving
like a wild wheatflower dancing,
waving in the softly breathing wind.
He watches her go weaving,
moving slowly through the moonlight,
and he fingers ripened grain in calloused hand.
There's just one thing to do now
that his daughter is departed:
to harvest cleanly and without regret.
In this way he pays homage
to the precious seeds he planted;
one blooms by rooting, one by blowing away.

vi: Advice for my Daughters

Advice for my Daughters

You are no stranger in this land
yet no one sees the world you wander in,
so look to the Earth for comfort
and like the lone birch tree,
embrace the moon.

The perfect hunter does not seek love
but wanders into the trees
armed with innocence.
If love comes,
she surrounds herself with stillness
and lets love move through her
like sunlight
through an open door.

To know yourself
pay no attention in school;
anyone can learn to be a fool.
Learn from mountains how to face death
with silence and patience.
Have no fear of death.
It is like the last song of the cricket
across the clear, bright frost:
a pause
and not a goodbye.

The Divorced Man Sings to His Daughter

I am half way through a lullaby
holding Little Wind in my arms,
with my torn rag of a voice
singing my heart out
in a torrent of off-key love.
Suddenly she is weeping deeply,
her heart spilling
like a spring creek in full flood.
She holds me,
kisses my homely face,
throws over all defense
and hands me her vulnerable heart;
her eyes are radiant with trust
like the face of God
creating a new man.
In that moment she creates me.

That was years ago.
Every moment since
has been one fool's effort
to be worthy of the crown
which a child of heaven
laid softly
at the door of his heart.

Ghazal for Mothers

I do not believe God is a woman.
He is a man with lovely, soft breasts.

Men call my loins the Mound of Venus;
they rhapsodize over what they understand least.

My womb is a great empty mystery.
Now the mystery fills me and kicks.

During delivery, my neck veins stand like chords
the awful pain is so fine.

The baby sleeps soundly on my belly.
If I could stop crying, I would laugh so loud.

On the third day after crucifixion Christ rose from the tomb;
on the third day after childbirth my breasts fill with milk.

Little Wind in Her Joy

At ten she is ancient and still,
sits alone on the porch
and watches the red moth
struggling in a web.
When the dark spider comes
the red wings flutter loud;
she kneels close,
makes no move to interfere.
Sunlight falls
and the red wing burns low, flickers
and goes out;
still she sits and watches.

Death will stalk the hunter and the prey,
will cast its web of dark across the day,
but will not catch the silent one
who sits and watches moon and sun
as they are born and then are borne away.

Wombman

Hers is the quiet room
where the unknown dons its costume
and enters the known world.
Hers is the solace
for one who wanders,
the comfort
for one who has lost The Way.
Hers is the gateway
between Heaven and Earth:
within Her, Nothing is;
through Her, everything comes;
between two movements
She is the rest.

We Drink With Cupped Hands

On our knees drinking with cupped hands
from our creek
is a kind of praying
for my daughters and me.
In time of drouth
there is nothing holier
than the water in the bowl of our hands
poured over our upraised faces
or sipped on bent knee,
giving thanks.
Religion is such a simple thing:
either it is cupping hands in deep gratitude
and filling them with creek water,
swallowing God whole,
or it is nothing at all.

Everything That Rises Falls Away

Beautiful daughters
I love to hold you in my arms
for just a moment
as our bodies fade away from us
like wonder from a child's eyes.

Your kisses are so dear to me.
They are complete:
no pretense, no expectation,
fleeting and full of grace.
They are like piano notes
heard soft across a lawn
at sunset:
so thin and quick
a quiver of beauty
in the dying light.

Beloveds, it is good to see
this latest shape our death takes:
you are aspens with oak-courage,
thin white dancers of moonlight,
slender love shimmering
in a tremble of wind and rain;

I am an old fool of a dog
shambling down a dirt road
in a cloud of dust, wondering   wondering
where have all the rabbits gone,
why does the day grow suddenly dim and cold,
can I make it to the aspen grove
and lie there softly as the darkness comes?

The Old Woman Teaches the Young Girl About Her Body

Grandmother, my breasts are so small,
she said as they sat in the hot spring.
The old woman said nothing at all
for a long time, just sat staring
at the trees through the rising steam.
The long quiet made it seem
she had not heard; she had of course.
Then she turned. These are not a source
of strength, she said with a touch
to the young girl's budding breast,
unless your heart is free
of desire, depends on no one. Such
a clear heart is a place of rest,
a source of strength, and loving harmony.
The heart of a free woman is the force
behind her beauty. Only remorse
will come to her who is in thrall
to fair face or full breast; she feels the sting
of time, old age is a gall.
But the free woman will sing
as old age beauties her and fills her heart;
her love will never fail her or depart,
not when death makes its claim on face and breast,
not when sun falls and Earth comes to its rest.

Little Wind

Beloved daughter this name chose you
for your marriage with the Earth;
it is a protection
for when you wear it
you will be invisible,
known only by your effect
on other living things.

Thus, the summer forest
moves and sways
as if it danced alone,
but it is you who spins
the living seeds away,
who scatters and collects
and makes the leaves to dance and sing.

And the naked winter trees
are nude for you
so that their bodies
as they wait alone in the forest
are deeply touched
by the breath of a lover
they cannot contain with limbs or desires.

Little Wind
you cool, you comfort,
you gather up the Earth and build;
you howl, you whirl,
you wear the Earth away;
you soar, you reach the sky.
You die. You spring up and fly.

Rain Drop

Beloved daughter this name chose you
because the Earth has a great thirst
and you are its living water
which all beings are come to drink.

You cause the seed in the field
to rise and flower,
you move the great stone
from the mountain top

to its rest in the swollen stream.
Within, you have no form, are not contained;
your outer will not fight
but takes the path which struggles least

and shapes itself
according to the need.
Your patience smooths stone,
carves canyon, whittles mountain,

carries bones to their decay.
You are the friend of Man,
the builder, the wearing away.
You fall. You rise again.

Epilogue

What the Old Cheyenne Women at Sand Creek Knew

All along the creek bank
they crouched holding the children
until the last warrior was dead
and the soldiers turned slowly toward them
like men in a bad dream.
The old women knew what was coming.
All along the creek bank
they tore off their shawls,
their shirts, their scarves,
anything close at hand
and they covered the eyes of the children.
The old women knew that if young children
saw what men in a bad dream could do
they would not die a clean death
so they covered the eyes of the children
and made no move to run.
The old women knew it was time.

All along the creek bank
they sat with their eyes wide open
watching and rocking the swaddled children
and when the soldiers opened fire
they tumbled into the creek,
the dead children in their arms
with eyes covered
so they would not see
what men in a bad dream could do.
All along the creek bank
the old women knew how to move
from one dream to another
and take the children safely through;
the old women knew
what men in a bad dream could do.

If you have enjoyed Red Hawk's poems, we invite you
to write for a complete list of books available in the
August House Poetry Series.

August House, Inc.
1010 West Third Street
Little Rock, Arkansas 72201
501-376-4516